She vs life.

Other books by Donna Owens:

Awaken Your Divine Goddess
Divine Goddess Journal
Divine Goddess Night Journal
365 Days of Healing Mantras
Yoga, My Bed & M.E.

Copyright © Donna Owens 2022
ISBN-13 : 979-8435820263

This content is intended for individual use only.
No content may be copied or used without written consent from Donna.

Artwork from Canva Pro

For Life, who writes these words
for you and I.

Introduction

She vs Life has been written to hold you in times of feeling broken, alone and when you feel it's you against the world.

This collection of personal thoughts and feelings were birthed from my own dark moment in life hoping for brighter days.

These pages and words are perfectly imperfect
raw and messy
up and down
just like our emotions
just like She
just like Life

I hope they hold your heart and comfort your soul.

She is Life

Here she stands
in a world where there are so many lost souls
deflated and exhausted
scared and confused
searching and pushing for answers
outside of themselves
she sees them
for <u>she is a lost soul too</u>

She is Life

When you find there is no light in your heart
these pages shall be the candle which flickers
with the whispers
"*Remember you are loved*"

She my Life

The world is full of broken hearts
let us help each other piece ourselves
back to whole again
for we are all walking jigsaw pieces
just longing and searching
to find the heart
that fits our soul

She vs Life

She can't see her path
as low clouds surround her soul
she can't tell the difference from the rain
and her tears which stream down her face
her heart is as heavy as the skies right now
she's lost in the haze of a dark winters day
hoping that she can once again
find the warmth within
guiding her back to brighter ways

She my Life

And if each star were a letter
I would align them so they shone

"You are not alone"

upon your darkest hour
to remind you of your beautiful divine power

She is Life

Look in the mirror
connect to your soul
despite the uncertainty
which weavers within your eyes
take a deep breath
and tell yourself

"I got this"

She vs Life

Sometimes there are no words to be told
on a cloudy day and that's okay
let yourself be
and breathe away the grey
for the clouds will eventually float away
leaving you once again
basking in the warmth of sunnier days

She is Life

The sun rises and smiles
and warms up her tender heart
melting away all the hurt
even if it's just for a brief moment

The sun sets and the world settles down
and despite her pain
she remembers to be grateful
and dream of a better tomorrow

She vs Life

Tonight
release the pressure you put on yourself
to have it all figured out
to release the grip of life
and allow life to be
what it's all meant to be

She vs Life

Oh how you want to break yourself free
but how
you are caught in the tangle
of your over-working
over-hurting heart

She vs Life

How do you break free from a web
which keeps you trapped
where you feel there is no hope of freedom
when you feel your wings are tightly wrapped
how do you break free

She my Life

There are days where she just doesn't know
she is tired and overwhelmed
by a life that's oh so cold
so she takes her heart
and her favourite mug of tea
and curls up in the comforting chair
with the sun on her soul
until she feels like herself once again

She my Life

Let me remind you
no matter what you are going through
right now
no matter what you are feeling

never
ever
give up
hope

She is Life

Rest
sit with the silence and uncertainty
Breathe
sit with your worries and write out your thoughts
Trust
it won't always be this way

She vs Life

Today I wish to feel like the successful future me
the woman who struts down the street in the clothes
which makes her feel like a million dollars
the woman with a smile on her face
who has a heart full of joy
from all the love that she pours out into the world
today I wish to her feel her
as I'm struggling to *be* her
so I'm going to put on my favourite dress
and strut down the street of dreams
where she's waiting for me

She vs Life

All she ever wanted was peace and love
in a world that didn't offer them
so she decided to give them to herself

She is Life

You are learning to surrender to faith
to find your own power and strength within
day by day
hour by hour
you know you're going to be okay
and will find your own perfect way

She vs Life

Life tells you to be yourself
but then tells to follow the rules of the masses
life tells you
you are wrong
too much
too little
that you are not doing it right
you forget who you truly are
you are scared to show who you truly are
so who are you truly
when life doesn't tell you who to be

She vs Life

Your emotions run wild
an unpredictable force
one moment you are the calm breeze
of a delicate spring morning
and the next a raging storm
of thunder and rain
in the bleak darkness of a cold winters night

She ws Life

In a world full of billions of people
you often feel lonely
looking for just one heart to call home
for you are tired
tired of fighting
this battle of life alone

She vs Life

You're human
with emotions as deep as the ocean
and as flowing and unpredictable as the waves
be gentle with your soul
as you learn to surf the waves of life

She vs Life

She craves to wake up to stillness
with sun beams opening her heart
she craves to sit and just be
before her day starts
she craves the slow morning pace
savouring the moment
in her coffee filled daze

She is Life

Her mornings are made for
her coffee
her heart
and she
allowing herself to just be
dancing barefoot to the song of her soul

She vs Life

You live in survival mode because that's the life
you have always known
to survive

She vs Life

This wasn't where she thought she would be
at this stage of her life
feeling like an abandoned child
out in the cold at her age
her life full of worries and strife
and where she doesn't know how to make it right
because as of now
her bright future seems so far out of sight

Side my Life

Where can you find *hope*
when you're lost in the fog of life
where can you find *trust*
in the midst of the dark night
where can you feel the *love*
when you are stranded in the cold
where can you find *anything*
when it all feels like it's been taken away

it's time to find them within

She vs Life

You know you can't stay here
here is feeling lost alone and scared
you have been here for far too long
you know it's time to move on
you know no-one is coming to save you
only you can save yourself
you know nothing will change if you stay here
you have to take a step
but which step will you take

She is Life

Suddenly life has kicked you out of the nest
you're scared
you don't know if you can fly
you feel abandoned and you feel hurt
you want the safety of the nest
of all that you knew
you are free falling
into the unknown
not sure how you'll survive
but you will
trust your wings
trust yourself
if you want to soar
than you will have to learn to fly

She is Life

You're tired of fighting to make life right
you're angry that you gave it your all
and still you're here
time and time again in the darkness of life
you want to give up
you feel you have nothing more to give
you scream silent screams in the still of the night
S u r r e n d e r
break and fall to your knees
life has planted you to grow
you were made to bloom bright

She is Life

Let the old fall away
as painful as it may be
know it is creating space for new things
to come your way
things that you might not see right now
things that may seem impossible
but trust and let go
for it is holding on that is hurting you so

She my Life

She didn't fit into the ways of the world
a life of pushing and striving to survive
she needed freedom
where her soul could dance
people laughed at her funny ways
but they lived a life full of stressful days
that wasn't for her
beccause her life was meant for more

She vs Life

Weak and tired
she sits on the corner of the life
wishing someone could show her which way to go
sat with the familiar feeling of being alone
exhausted from trying to stay so strong
the weight of her emotions
has brought her to this space
wishing to see a familiar loving face

She vs Life

Empty
she feels she has nothing left
exhausted from trying and hurting from being
kicked down by strife
her heavy heart and her tear stained face
she sits and wonders

"will I *ever* succeed at this game of life"

She vs Life

There *is* life after the storm
where all that you had was torn away
somehow you will build the new
from all your tears
and the shattered broken pieces of your heart
you *will* find a brand new start

She vs Life

Oh how to fly free like the birds
when you feel your wings are clipped
and you're bound to the ground

She my Life

In the vast darkness of the midnight sky
there are millions of stars that twinkle

"Don't give up"

She vs Life

It's okay if today you don't have a lot to say
curl up and watch the clouds go by
tomorrow is another day

She my Life

One day you will stop waiting
and focus on your own sweet self
but until that day
stay gentle with your soul
each step of the way

She my Life

It is always in silence
that your pain screams the loudest
where your fears run around wild and untamed
where you have no where to run
and no where to hide

She is My Life

You feel like the universe
has taken everything away
that it's not on your side
and you have no idea
how you're going to make it through
take my hand
open your heart and
T R U S T

She vs Life

This lost feeling will pass
they always do
it's okay to feel lost empty and emotional
hold yourself as you move through each day
you are shifting to a new chapter new growth
and a new you

She my Life

Another day fades to shades of pale pink and blue
as shadows of fear start to
brush gently through your hair
the darkness feels impending
but you are a star
burning and shining
in the stillness of the dark midnight air

She vs Life

They were everything which you needed
but they broke your spirit
took your heart and scarred it
with their name

o v e r

a n d o v e r

a n d o v e r

a g a i n

She is Life

You may be broken
but you aren't beaten
for the vision you have
for yourself and your life
is the reason to keep on going

She vs Life

I know it's been hard
those months of hurt and pain have slowly
taken their toll on your heart
but here is your space
for your brand new start

She vs Life

Step by small step
one breath at a time
keep moving forward
soon the fog will lift
soon you will find clarity
soon you will see how far you have come
soon your future will be your present
a gift to cherish and hold

She is Life

Breathe
Surrender your mind from the fear
breathe
just let it be
for what it's meant to be
open your heart to faith
breathe
for what's meant to be
will be
and it will soon be yours
you'll see

She my Life

Roar out your sacred anger
let your tears break free
hold space for your emotions
to be heard felt and to be seen
ground your being into this moment
take your sacred fire into your loving hands
and in this tender embrace you can nurture
your rage back to love

She vs Life

Be easy with yourself
you are forever learning healing
discovering and evolving
be easy with yourself when you feel lost
be easy with yourself when you feel overwhelmed
be easy with yourself when you are hurting
just be easy with yourself

She my Life

You deserve to heal
to say goodbye to the past
it's time to hold your head up high
don't go back
look at the scars that's tattooed
upon your heart
move on my love
remember the pain
it's time to let the past ghosts lie

She is Life

It seems impossible right now
that you can't see your future in sight
but trust the wisdom of your heart
to guide you out of the darkness
and into the light

She is Life

Saying goodbye to the old that you knew
is hard
leaving things places people and pieces
of your heart that you have outgrew
but having the courage to say hello to the new
is where you bloom and find your new home

She is Life

She is yearning for the spark of hot summer days
to come back into her heart
the comfort of the glowing sun to radiate her soul
just like summer
she is yearning to shine again

She vs Life

That is your power
you'll keep going
keep trying
keep falling
keep getting up
and keep believing
until you get to where you want to be

She vs Life

You are tired
tired of not being chosen
tired of not being seen
tired of not being heard
by others
by life

it is time to choose yourself

She my Life

All the flowing rivers of tears that you have cried
all the thunderous storms of life that
you have had to ride
all the minutes of loneliness that you have endured
y o u a r e s t i l l h e r e
look at how strong you are
look at what you have over come so far
i'm proud of you

She my Life

How can you trust your heart
and hear its whispers in the wind
begin to feel the earth beneath your feet
know that you are held
begin to hear the echoes of the trees
know that you are guided
begin to trust in the unseen
know that you are safe

She is Life

Life is but a story
full of chapters of love and pain
uncertainty lessons and blessings
a story of healing and over-coming
and that is a story to share to help heal others

She vs Life

After the breakdown
comes the breakthrough
while you feel you can't go on
keep going
it always feels the hardest and darkest
right before the breakthrough
so hold on my dear
for your breakthrough is coming

She vs Life

We are only here for a brief moment
make the moment count
before it becomes just a memory

She my Life

And here I am feeling like I'm being buried alive
as the universe slowly pours the earth over my
spirit to be buried in darkness
but I *will* rise
like the bright shining yellow flower in the sun
who broke through the crack of the pavement
reminding me I'm strong
and that anything is possible

She of Life

It's lonely isn't it
finding your way
people come and people go
in a moment you can feel peace
and in the next confusion
things that once rang true
has now left for something new
but don't stop finding your way
for those who are meant to walk with you
will find you
it's true

She my Life

It's okay to grieve yesterday and the memories
it is okay to wish to be still there
it's okay to cry all the hurt
of the loss of what was
for they were all important moments that are
forever etched into your heart

She vs Life

She needed to leave
to breathe

She vs Life

Hold on
life changes like the seasons
sometimes without notice
or even without a reason
hold on

She vs Life

An anxious mind always creeps up
and tries to tear you down
so in those moments
know to come home
to hold yourself with love

She vs Life

That was just who she was
too nice
too kind
she waited for people for too long
she gave when all they did was take
she dropped her life to be there for those who
didn't drop anything to be there when she
needed them
and it hurt

why was having such a big kind heart
so painful

She vs Life

Where was her happily ever after
which life promised her
how much longer did she have to wait

She my Life

Life moves so quickly
within a blink of an eye all the years of her being
carefree had gone
oh how to get them back
to still be young
to have exciting plans
and to live with no worries about tomorrow

She my Life

Don't people care anymore
far too busy with their own life to see
how her quietness is a soft gentle plea
for love
a shoulder
and a hug
please don't mistake her quietness
for being busy
for she is simply waiting
to see who reaches out their hand and cares

She is Life

Even in a room full of people
she feels all alone
even with the sound of laugher
she still cries silent tears
for her soul is deflated
her spirit feels trapped
she is just needing to find others
who lights her heart up

She is Life

If you are struggling with something right now
know that you have the love strength
and courage to be okay
to be more than okay
you have the power to rise
you have the power to face another day

She is Life

Every time
you opened your heart to love
they broke you
you gave too many chances
and they still didn't change
you are hurting yourself
reliving the pain

She vs Life

Loneliness hits you
each time you're left out in the cold
everyone else is all too busy and cosy
everyone seems to have someone to hold
even though you smile and say you are okay
you long so much for company and plans
and the warmth of tender loving hands
you don't like feeling invisible
but you always are
the loner of life

She is Life

When did life become so hard
was this all that life had to offer
pain and loneliness
exhaustion and worry
why can't life give you a break
what did you do to deserve all of this
where was your life full of happiness
love and bliss

She vs Life

You find it hard to believe that life will shine again
you have sat in the depth of the rain for so long now
that you have almost given up hope
the rain can't pour forever
can it

She vs Life

She knows
she'll get back on track
that she'll pick herself up and get on with it
she always does
because she has a heart of gold
and soul made of steel

She vs Life

All she wants is for someone to hold her
and to tell her that everything will be more than
okay

She vs Life

Know that you don't need
to have it all figured out
you don't need to have solid plans
or follow the crowd
right now
just be
and breathe

She vs Life

Life was never about finding love
but instead about being love
giving love
loving life and loving yourself
then you have love
everywhere you go

She is Life

You are capable and more than enough
life might not be going how you planned
but trust in yourself to navigate your way
and know that you are deeply loved

She vs Life

The lies in which fairytales made you believe
that in the middle of your dark hour some
knight will sweep in to save the day
the truth is
no one is coming to save you
you have to be your own saving knight

She vs Life

                                    She's trying
                                    she really is
                            to change her ways
                          she wants to be okay
                     she wants to be secure and
           to hold herself through the heavier days
but why is what she's doing never seems enough
         for whatever she tries never seems to work
"oh please universe give this tired heart a break"

She vs Life

Life has stopped moving
each day is the same
tired of trying
exhausted from crying
she doesn't know what to do
to get her life moving once more

She vs Life

She often sat and watched the people pass
walking and wounded each in their own way
all hiding their pain with a smile
as they continued to walk each life mile

She vs Life

Despite the hardships of life
please remember how precious it is
cherish each memory and the people you love
because it's only ever the memories that you
will ever have

She vs Life

The game had changed
love wasn't the same
digital romance was a painful game
people weren't looking for hearts but instead
wanting hits
she had enough of ghosting and being left on read
tired of being an option
all she wanted was just to be their favourite
notification

She vs Life

Could she cry anymore
it's all she seems to be doing these days
her heart is heavy and sore
she has cried a million tears in just a few hours
which have seemed to last for years
she feels broken and beaten
not able to find anything
to guide her out of the sea of hopelessness
in which her heart was weeping

She vs Life

She wasn't lazy
it was the fact she had always been made to feel
incapable
it was her truama response to
"why bother"

She vs Life

And in a blink of an eye they were gone
she opened her heart to love
and suddenly the love was gone
she's now scared to love so fully again

She my Life

It's okay you lost yourself for a while
trying to find all that you need in the external world
people and places you wanted home
you wanted love
you wanted security
you wanted happiness
you wanted others to offer these to you
and there you stood
left homeless and hurt
please don't close your heart
or let it grow cold
it's not about shutting love out
it's about loving yourself first

She vs Life

Rage and rain that's all she ever knew these days
like a storm
she didn't know the chaos of her emotions
how they were wrecking havoc on her soul

She is Life

She always worried
did she do enough
if only they knew just how much she cared for them
how she would do anything to keep their heart safe

She vs Life

She was still waiting to truly live
to truly laugh
and to truly love

She is Life

Life is a flow
one day it rains
and you are soaked in despair
the next it's sunny
and you feel everything
is bright and right

She is Life

She always had a heart full of hope
unfortunately it was always hopeful that the
wrong people would change their ways

She vs Life

Then one day you will wake up
and something has shifted
you'll feel a lightness in your heart and a deep
knowing you deserve more
you will commit to yourself that you won't
settle for less anymore

She is Life

She needed to stop searching for love
in the wrong places and faces
chasing to be held and to be supported
she needed to stop
for only she could hold
and love all of her broken pieces

She is Life

She was lonely
wanting to find the place
where she truly belonged
a space where she could truly come alive
without a map and no one around
she hoped the light of her heart would show
her the way

She vs Life

The one person who she wanted to hold
the most in the darkness of her night
wasn't there to hold her tight

She vs Life

The black midnight sky isn't empty
for it is full of twinkling opportunities and
possibilities for those who are willing to believe
in stardust and magic

She is Life

Do you remember
when you used to dance with the daisies
in the sun
barefoot in the fields of the warm green grass
a care free spirit spinning in cotton dresses and
hair in messy plaits
laughing and skipping with the butterflies
fluttering around your hat
oh to be that joyful maiden once more

She vs Life

Somedays you are flying high
and other times you can't leave the ground
it's okay to rest your wings
settle into the earth and ground you soul
deepen your breath
soon you will be back to soaring the skies

She vs Life

Let it all go
holding on is causing you pain
don't be afraid of the empty space
for the universe will fill it with the love that you deserve

She is Life

Sometimes you are isolated to find and
befriend and love yourself first
to love your own company
to discover your true self

She is Life

The truth is
she is deeply lonely
in this over-crowded world

She is Life

She is dancing this journey of life as are you
she stumbles and falls
she skips and she spins
sometimes she dances in the rain
and sometimes in the sun beams
sometimes through tears
and sometimes with a grin
but through it all
she continues to dance
and so shall you

She is Life

With the falling of the old leaves
which danced down around her
she released a sigh of relief
for she too was also ready
to let the old just fall and dance away

She my Life

Don't think you're not heard
in the chaos of the world
your tender whispers are the peace souls seek
soft and soothing
calm and compassionate
keep whispering your heart
for those who feel weak

She vs Life

That girl with the fragile heart
she took her broken pieces
and turned them into art
she nurtured her hurt
hour by hour
and became the woman
who turned her pain into her power

She ov Life

She decided to write her own fairytale
full of chapters of peace, passion and wellness
and today was page one

to be continued......

Let's share the love
If my words touched your soul
be sure to share them for others
tag me @divine_feminine_writer
@she_vs_life

Acknowledgements

I want to truly thank life and the dark moments it gifted me over the past year which birthed these words to light.

For every soul who loves, supports and shares my art thank you, thank you, thank you.

And as always, for my daughter Mollie.
Your light, your smile, your heart and wit inspires me every day to be the best person I can be in the world.

About Donna

Donna Owens is an author and writer who weaves life into words to nurture and empower women all over the world with her books.

Contact Donna on her Instagram
@divine_feminine_writer
@she_vs_life
www.donna-owens.com

Printed in Great Britain
by Amazon